CONTENTS

CHAPTER 1

Afghanistan – An Overview

Afghanistan is a mountainous country in central Asia. In the most recent episode of its turbulent history, Afghanistan's people have experienced 27 years of war and their troubles are not yet over. Afghanistan is famous for having been ruled by a regime known as the Taliban, which enforced its own strict version of Islam and sheltered the Islamic fundamentalist leader Osama bin Laden from 1996.

A STRATEGIC POSITION

For the Afghan people, the Taliban were simply the most recent in a long line of rulers and conquerors. For centuries, control of Afghanistan has been regarded as essential for the domination of the whole of central Asia. Many people have risked their lives travelling the treacherous routes through Afghanistan's high mountain passes to battle for conquest of the country. Afghanistan's strategic position along the ancient 'Silk Route' (see page 34), and sandwiched between the Middle East, central Asia and the Indian subcontinent, made the prize worth the difficult journey for Genghis Khan, Alexander the Great, the Persians, the British and the Soviet Union.

▼ The Bamiyan Buddhas in 1998, before they were destroyed by the Taliban.

Afghanistan

NIKKI VAN DER GAAG

WAYLAND

First published in 2007 by Wayland

Copyright © 2007 Wayland

This paperback edition published in 2009 by Wayland, a division of Hachette Children's Books, an Hachette UK Company
338 Euston Road, London NW1 3BH. www.hachette.co.uk

Wayland Australia, Hachette Children's Books, Level 17/207 Kent Street, Sydney, NSW 2000

Commissioning editor: Nicola Edwards
Editor: Patience Coster
Inside design: Chris Halls, www.mindseyedesign.co.uk
Cover design: Wayland
Series concept and project management by EASI-Educational Resourcing
(info@easi-er.co.uk)
Statistical research: Anna Bowden
Maps and graphs: Martin Darlison, Encompass Graphics

Printed and bound in China

British Library Cataloguing in Publication Data
Gaag, Nikki van der
    Afghanistan. - (World in focus)
    1. Afghanistan - Juvenile literature
    I. Title
    958.1'047

ISBN: 978-0-7502-5921-7

Cover top: This beautiful mosque in Mazar-e-Sharif is a shrine to Hazrat Ali, cousin and son-in-law of the Prophet Mohammed.
Cover bottom: A woman attends an adult literacy class in Hesarak village, northern Afghanistan.
Title page: A meeting to elect members of the Loya Jirga, or Grand Council, takes place in Mazar-e Sharif in December 2003.

The author would like to thank Ali Askari for his research.

The author and publisher would like to thank the following for allowing their pictures to be reproduced in this publication: Corbis 8 (Stapleton Collection), 9 (Mimmo Jodice), 13 (Rahmat Gul/epa), 15 (Francois Carrel/Montagne Magazine), 17 (Reuters), 19 (Corbis Sygma/Patrick Robert), 20 (Michael S. Yamashita), 22 (Ron Sachs/CNP), 24 (epa), 25 (David Bathgate), 26 (Corbis Sygma/Silva Joao), 27 (Corbis Sygma/Christian Simonpietri), 28 (Stephanie Sinclair), 33 (Adrees Latif/Reuters), 34 (Reuters), 47 (David Bathgate), 49 (Ahmad Masood/Reuters), 56 (DLILLC), 59 (Syed Jan Sabawoon/epa); EASI-Images/Jenny Matthews 4, 5, 6, 10, 11, 12, 14, 16, 18, 21, 23 and title page, 29, 30, 31, 32, 35, 36, 37, 38, 39, 40, 41, 42, 43, 44, 45, 46, 48, 50, 51, 52, 53, 54, 55, 57, 58.

The website addresses (URLs) included in this book were valid at the time of going to press. However, because of the nature of the Internet, it is possible that some addresses may have changed or sites may have changed or closed down since publication. While the author and publishers regret any inconvenience this may cause the readers, no responsibility for any such changes can be accepted by either the author or the publishers.

The directional arrow portrayed on the map on page 7 provides only an approximation of north.

The data used to produce the graphics and data panels in this title were the latest available at the time of production. The political situation in Afghanistan at the time of going to press means that only limited data is available.

▲ Young women attend a tailoring class in Ufimalik village. Projects such as this help give people the opportunity to find work and avoid poverty.

Afghanistan has a rich culture dating back thousands of years. It is home to the remnants of the huge 2,000-year-old Bamiyan Buddhas which were destroyed by the Taliban in 2001. It was the birthplace of Zoroaster, who founded the Zoroastrian fire religion, and home to poet-philosopher Jelauddin Rumi (lived 1207-73) and the famous scientist and philosopher Avicenna (lived 980-1037).

RICH – AND POOR

Afghanistan is a country rich in resources as well as history. It has gems, gold, copper, coal, iron ore, gas and oil. It is also a country with many different ethnic groups – the main ones are Pashtun, Hazara, Tajik and Uzbek – among which more than 30 languages are spoken.

However, many of Afghanistan's resources have only been discovered since the 1960s, and the terrain, climate and years of war mean that few have been extracted. Instead, there has been a thriving trade in opium poppies. Afghanistan is the world's largest producer of opium, from which the drug heroin is made. It is also one of the poorest countries in the world. The average life expectancy today is only about 43 years, and one child in four dies before the age of five.

Twenty-seven years of war and repression have left the country's infrastructure badly damaged, its economy in tatters and its people living in poverty. There are frequent breaks in the delivery of the power supply, even in the capital city of Kabul, which make daily life difficult. Afghanistan is a dangerous country to live in, and many areas are seeing the return of Taliban fighters. The Afghans are a proud and resilient people, but improving their lives and setting their country on the road to a better future will not be easy.

Physical geography

- Land area: 647,500 sq km/250,000 sq miles
- Water area: 0 sq km/0 sq miles
- Total area: 647,500 sq km/250,000 sq miles
- World rank (by area): 42
- Land boundaries: 5,529 km/3,436 miles
- Border countries: China, Iran, Pakistan, Tajikistan, Turkmenistan, Uzbekistan
- Coastline: 0 km/0 miles (landlocked)
- Highest point: Noshaq (7,485 m/24,557 ft)
- Lowest point: Amu Darya (258 m/846 ft)

Source: CIA World Factbook

 Did you know?

Afghanistan is one of the most heavily mined countries in the world (see page 55). There are landmines in all but two provinces, most of them laid during the time when the Soviets occupied the country. There are many people who have had their arms and legs blown off as a result of stepping on landmines.

▲ A woman walks along a road through a heavily landmined area near Bagram. The marker stones show the safest way through the minefield.

UZBEKISTAN

KYRGYZSTAN

CHINA

TAJIKISTAN

TURKMENISTAN

IRAN

Amu Darya

38°   38°

70°

72°   74°

PAMIRS

Panj

74°

66°

68°

Jeyretan

Aqchah

Balkh

Kunduz

Faizabad

Mazar-e Sharif

Kholm

Taliqan

Khanabad

▲ Noshaq
7,485 m

64°

Aybak

Baghlan

H I N D U   K U S H

36°

36°

Meymaneh

Balkh

Nahrin

TORKESTAN MOUNTAINS

HESAR MOUNTAINS

Kunduz

Salang ⋈
Pass

Qaleh-ye Now

SAFID MOUNTAIN RANGE

Bamiyan

KABUL ★

Asadabad

62°

Hari Rud

Pagman

Sarobi

Jalalabad

34°

Ghurian

Herat

BABA MOUNTAINS

Bagram

Kabul

Khyber Pass ⋈
1,072m

34°

AFGHANISTAN

Gardez

Helmand

Ghazni

70°

Khowst

32°

Farah

Oruzgan

Lawrah

32°

*Sistan
Lake*

Gereshk

68°

Lashkar Gah

Kandahar

PAKISTAN

Zaranj

*ZEREH
DEPRESSION*

Helmand

RIGESTAN

30°

30°

*MARGOW
DESERT*

62°

66°

64°

INDIA

Legend

★ Capital

● Cities > 250,000

● Cities > 100,000

• other cities

▲ Mountain

⋈ Pass

N

0   200   400 kilometres

0   100   200 miles

History

Afghanistan's history dates back more than 5,000 years. As a result of its strategic location, Afghanistan has been a battleground for the many peoples who have struggled for possession of its mountainous terrain.

ANCIENT AFGHAN EMPIRES

People have been living in Afghanistan since 5,000 BC. The region became part of the Persian Empire when conquered by Darius the Great (521-486 BC). In 329 BC, the Macedonian military commander Alexander the Great (356-323 BC) ousted the Persians. Reminders of his rule can still be found today. Many towns, for example, are built on Greek foundations.

From the first to the middle of the fifth century AD, a Buddhist civilization ruled the ancient kingdom of Gandhara, which stretched from eastern Afghanistan to north-west Pakistan. Buddhist art and culture reached its peak with the accession of King Kanishka to the throne (AD 100-144) and Buddhist kings reigned in the city of Bamiyan, in the heart of the Hindu Kush mountains, until the tenth century.

In 962, invading Arabs began the Ghaznavid dynasty and introduced Islam to the country. In the thirteenth century, Afghanistan was conquered by the Mongolian warrior, Genghis Khan (c.1162-1227). He conquered most of central Asia, through lands that are now Afghanistan, Tajikistan, Uzbekistan and Turkmenistan, and westward into what is now Turkey. In 1273, the Venetian merchant Marco Polo crossed Afghanistan on his voyage from Italy to China to discover the Silk Route, which had once been the main way to travel between Europe, the Near East, India and China (see page 34).

In 1370, the Mongol warrior Tamerlane (c.1336-1405), who claimed his descent from Genghis Khan, became the next in a long line of conquerors. His descendants continued to

 Did you know?

Tamerlane was called 'Timur the Lame' by Europeans because of his limp. His leg had been injured when he was a child.

◀ A painting from an old manuscript shows Genghis Khan outside his tent.

◀ An ancient mosaic of Alexander the Great, who drove the Persians out of Afghanistan in 329 BC.

rule the area until the Persians took over in 1550. They also founded the Moghul Empire in India. The next two hundred years saw constant warfare with Persia. In 1750, King Ahmad Shah Abdali established the Kingdom of Afghanistan. At its height, this stretched from the city of Delhi in the east to the Arabian Sea in the south.

Focus on: The city of Balkh

Balkh, the oldest city in Afghanistan, is known locally as the 'Mother of Cities'. Originally called Bactria, its origins date back many thousands of years, and it has been home to Buddhists, Jews and Muslims. Zoroaster, founder of the Zoroastrian religion of fire, is said to be buried here, and the philosopher-scientist Avicenna was born here in AD 980. Balkh was sacked by Genghis Khan in 1220 and again in the fourteenth century by Tamerlane.

THE NINETEENTH CENTURY

In the nineteenth century, Afghanistan became involved in rivalry between Britain and Russia, who both wanted control of the country. Between 1839 and 1842, the British fought the Afghans in what became known as the First Afghan War. They installed Shah Shuja as a puppet king but he was assassinated in 1842. The Afghan leader, Dost Mohammed Khan, drove back the British and declared himself king. The war ended in disastrous defeat for Britain.

In 1878, in the Second Afghan War, the British backed a new king, Abdul Rahman Khan, who remained on the throne until his death in 1901. The British withdrew from Afghanistan, but continued to control its foreign affairs and supply arms. In 1893, the Durand Line fixed the borders of Afghanistan and British India, splitting up Afghan tribal areas and leaving many Afghans in what is now Pakistan.

INDEPENDENCE

In 1919, following the First World War, increasing numbers of Afghans wanted independence from Britain. The Afghan king, Habibullah, was assassinated because of his support for the British. His son, Amanullah Shah, then declared independence. This was immediately recognized by Russia and, after a month of fighting (the Third Afghan War), by Britain. Amanullah Shah instituted reforms, but they proved controversial, and in 1928 he was forced to abdicate. In 1930, Nadir Khan took the throne and continued some of the reforms, but was assassinated in 1933. His son, Mohammed Zahir Shah, succeeded him and went on to develop a constitutional monarchy and tried to modernize the country. In 1959, women were allowed to enrol at universities and to take jobs outside the home. However, in 1973 and with Russia's support, Zahir Shah's cousin, Daoud Khan, staged a coup, proclaiming the country a republic and himself president.

THE SOVIET UNION INVADES

In 1978, Daoud was killed in a coup staged by the communist People's Democratic Party of Afghanistan (PDPA). Party chief Nur Mohammed Taraki became president and signed a treaty of friendship with the Soviet Union. At the same time, the Afghan guerrilla movement was born. Its members were known as the *mujahideen*, a word that has been used more generally since that time for those who fight for an Islamic cause. In 1979, the Soviet army invaded Afghanistan and massacred hundreds of peasants. The *mujahideen* started to attack the Soviet troops and, in the fighting that followed, the US ambassador and Taraki were both killed. The previously exiled communist leader Babrak Karmal took power.

▼ A young girl stands in front of a wrecked Soviet tank in Kabul in 1996. The war between the Soviet Union and the *mujahideen* destroyed many buildings in the city.

▶ Young women from a local militia organized by the Soviet Union to fight the *mujahideen* pose with their weapons.

The Soviets feared that the USA would attempt to assert its influence in Afghanistan. Therefore, in December 1979, the Soviet government under President Brezhnev sent in troops to fight the *mujahideen* and support Karmal. There was nationwide resistance to the Soviet invasion. Tens of thousands of *mujahideen* were trained in Pakistan and funded by the USA, Saudi Arabia and China. The US Central Intelligence Agency (CIA) began giving aid covertly to the *mujahideen*. Millions of Afghans fled to refugee camps in Pakistan. Soviet forces controlled the country's government and resources, and bombed the countryside, destroying villages and killing thousands of people.

From 1980-86, the CIA provided US$2 billion in military aid to the *mujahideen*, who were also funding their war through the opium trade. US President Ronald Reagan's National Security Decision Directive 166 called for efforts to drive the Soviets from Afghanistan 'by all means available'. In 1987, Mohammed Najibullah, head of the Afghan secret police, was installed as president. Finally, under an agreement signed in Geneva, the Soviet army withdrew in 1988. Nearly two million Afghans had lost their lives and six million had been made refugees. 15,000 Soviet troops had been killed.

THE FIGHT FOR KABUL

Despite the Soviet withdrawal, the fighting continued. Many people were opposed to Najibullah. Different warlords controlled different areas of the country, and were supported by different foreign backers. Afghanistan was breaking apart, and the United Nations (UN) failed to get the various sides to agree. In 1992, the four main factions of warlords – Dostum, Massoud/Rabbani, Hekmatyar and Hizb-i-Wahdat – fought for control of the Afghan capital, Kabul. Around a million people fled the city, 20,000 were killed and many became refugees.

ENTER THE TALIBAN

In 1994, a new force known as the Taliban was born in Afghanistan. Many of its leaders were *mujahideen* who had formerly been funded by the West to drive the Soviet Union from their country. The Taliban took the city of Kandahar, then Herat and, in 1996, captured Kabul and executed Najibullah. Its members were driven by a strict version of Islam. They imposed Sharia law on the country, banning women from working or going outdoors without a man, and forcing them to dress in an all-encompassing garment called the *burqa*. They closed girls' schools and insisted that all men grow beards. They banned television, music and art and destroyed many ancient treasures, including the Buddhas of Bamiyan.

In 1998, US cruise missiles were fired at alleged terrorist training camps in Afghanistan. The USA stated that this was retaliation for the destruction of American embassies in Kenya and Tanzania by local members of an Islamic organization called Al-Qaeda (see box opposite on Osama bin Laden). Iran sent thousands of troops to the Afghan border, and threatened to invade to stop the Taliban's 'ethnic cleansing' of Afghanistan's Shi'a Muslim minority. By 2000, the Taliban controlled around 80 per cent of Afghanistan. Only Pakistan, Saudi Arabia and the United Arab Emirates recognized it as a legitimate government.

In 2001, the Taliban tortured and killed hundreds of Hazaras (see pages 18-19) in Yakaolang. In the same year, the military leader Ahmad Shah Masoud of the Northern Alliance (a force made up of those in Afghanistan opposed to the Taliban) was killed by suicide bombers posing as journalists.

▼ This is what women under the Taliban would have seen through their *burqas*, which covered them from head to toe with only a small gap to look through.

▶ In September 2005, a woman from Jalalabad votes in the National Assembly elections.

11 SEPTEMBER AND THE INVASION

On 11 September 2001, four airliners were hijacked by 19 terrorists. Two of the airliners were deliberately flown into the World Trade Center in New York, the third was flown into the Pentagon in Washington DC and the fourth crashed into a field. Around 3,000 people died in the attacks. The Al-Qaeda organization, headed by the Saudi Arabian millionaire Osama bin Laden, claimed responsibility for the attacks. The world's attention was once again focused on Afghanistan, where the Taliban were sheltering bin Laden. The Taliban would not hand him over to the US authorities or reveal where he was hiding. US and Allied forces invaded the country, saying they wanted to root out the terrorists and their supporters. The Taliban were driven out of power in Afghanistan, but neither their leader, Mullah Mohammed Omar, nor Osama bin Laden were found. An estimated 3,000-3,400 civilians were killed in the fighting.

In 2001, a conference in Bonn, Germany, established a process for political rebuilding. Hamid Karzai was made interim president. In 2004, he became the first democratically elected president of Afghanistan. Elections for seats in the new government's legislative body, the National Assembly, were held in September 2005.

Focus on: Osama bin Laden

Osama bin Laden was born in 1957, and is linked with Afghanistan because he was one of the *mujahideen* who fought against the Soviet Union in the 1970s when it occupied the country. He supported the Taliban and shared their goal of creating an Islamic state in Afghanistan. In return, the Taliban allowed bin Laden to fund training camps in the country and hid him when he was charged with international terrorism. Osama bin Laden is supposedly the founder of Al-Qaeda, the Islamist organization that has carried out a number of terrorist attacks, including the 11 September bombings in the USA. He remains in hiding despite many attempts to find him.

 Did you know?

The word 'Taliban' comes from the Persian and Pashtun word *talib*, or religious student.

CHAPTER 3

Landscape and Climate

Afghanistan is shaped like a clenched fist, with its thumb stuck out to the north-east. It covers an area of around 647,500 sq km (around 250,000 sq miles), about the size of the US state of Texas. Its maximum length from west to east is about 1,240 km (770 miles); from north to south it is about 1,015 km (630 miles). It borders China, Iran, Pakistan, Tajikistan, Turkmenistan and Uzbekistan, but has no access to the sea. It is dominated by its mountains, which take up about half the country and divide it into three regions: the Central Highlands, the Northern Plains, and the South-western Plateau.

▲ A bright sun shines over the snow-capped mountains of the Hindu Kush. The mountains make it difficult to travel around Afghanistan.

Did you know?

At 7,485 m (24,557 ft) above sea level, Noshaq (or Nowshak) is the highest mountain in Afghanistan. It is also the second highest (after Tirich Mir in Pakistan) of the Hindu Kush range, which marks the border between Pakistan and Afghanistan. A Japanese team first climbed Noshaq in 1960.

A LAND OF EXTREMES

Most of Afghanistan has a sub-arctic mountain climate with dry, cold winters. In the Central Highlands, summer temperatures sometimes soar to 49°C (120°F). The Northern Plains cover around 64,000 sq km (24,700 sq miles) of

Did you know?

There are many glaciers and year-round snowfields in the mountains, and the extreme cold weather makes it impossible to go to school in the winter months in these areas. On many days, people cannot go out at all because it is too cold and the snow is too deep. Midwinter temperatures as low as -9°C (16°F) are common above 2,000 m (6,562 ft).

very fertile plains and hills. This is where most of the country's farming occurs, and where minerals and natural gas have been found. In the south-west of the country, there are high plateaux and sandy deserts (the South-western Plateau). The soil is mostly infertile and the climate dry and mild. In the western and southern regions, strong winds of up to 180 kph (112 mph) occur between June and September. They are known as the 'Winds of 120 Days' and can bring sand or dust storms.

▼ Climbers on a glacier on Mount Noshaq: the summit of the mountain (7,485 m/24,557 ft) can be seen in the distance.

Most of the rain in the country falls between the months of October and April. The amount of rain varies: the deserts receive less than 100 mm (4 in) of rain a year, whereas the mountains receive more than 1,000 mm (40 in), mostly as snow.

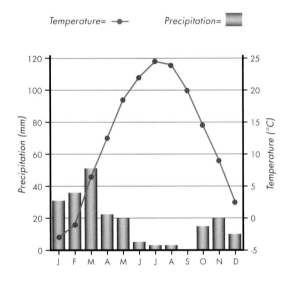

▲ Average monthly climate conditions in Kabul

RIVERS AND LAKES

Mountain streams feed many of Afghanistan's major rivers. The Amu Darya is the only river on which boats can sail. The Hari Rud River forms part of the border with Iran, and the Helmand River is used extensively for irrigation and agriculture. The Kabul River flows east into Pakistan to join the Indus River, which empties into the Indian Ocean. There are only a few small lakes. They include Zarkol, Shiveh, and the saline Lake Istadeh-ye Moqor, located south of the city of Ghazni.

EARTHQUAKES

Earthquakes are common in Afghanistan – there have been more than 1,300 recorded in its history since AD 734. This is because the

▼ A boy hurries across a swaying bridge over the Kabul River near Sarobi. Many people live alongside these rivers, where the land is more fertile than on the dry plains.

country lies on the southern fringe of the Eurasian tectonic plate, subject to collision with the Arabian plate to the south and the Indian plate to the south-east. Major earthquakes occurred in 1998, 2002, 2004 and 2005.

▼ A girl screams as she is held by her father during the powerful aftershock from an earthquake in Nahrin in the Hindu Kush. More than 2,000 people died and 30,000 were made homeless in the earthquake that struck in March 2002.

Focus on: Mountain passes

Mountain passes, some of them extremely narrow, have been vital entry and exit points for those trying to conquer Afghanistan. Alexander the Great invaded the country through the Kushan Pass in the west and left it through the Khyber Pass in the east to invade India. The Moghul emperor, Babur, used the same passes to conquer both Afghanistan and India in the 1500s. During the Afghan wars in the nineteenth and twentieth centuries, many battles were fought in the Khyber Pass. The most famous was in January 1842, when 16,000 British and Indian troops were killed. The British constructed a road through the pass in 1879. A railroad was also built there in the 1920s. The Salang Pass, with its Soviet-built tunnel, was one of the main routes the Soviets used to invade Afghanistan in 1979.

CHAPTER 4

Population and Settlements

In 2008 there were 32.7 million people in Afghanistan. Most people live in the countryside and 44.6 per cent of the population are under the age of 14. The reason for this is partly because people do not live long; the harsh climate, poverty and war mean that average life expectancy is just 44 years. This means that Afghanistan has one of the lowest life expectancies in the world.

ETHNIC GROUPS

Afghanistan has four main ethnic groups and a number of smaller ones. The Pashtuns, or Pushtuns, make up the largest group, at 42 per cent of the population. They are followed by the Tajiks at 27 per cent, and the Hazaras and the Uzbeks at 9 per cent each. Smaller groups include the Aimak, Turkmen and Baluchi. The different groups are related to many of the ethnic groups in Iran, Pakistan, Tajikistan, Turkmenistan and Uzbekistan. Many Pashtuns, for example, also live in north-western Pakistan, where they are called Pathans.

In Afghanistan, these ethnic or tribal groupings define who a person is and are therefore very important. Historically, there has been rivalry and fighting between the different groups and sometimes within them too. Traditionally, the Pashtuns have been the dominant group. They speak Pashto, which is one of the two official languages of Afghanistan. They have a tribal code called *pashtunwali,* which emphasizes courage, honour and hospitality. Hamid Karzai, who was elected president in 2004, is a Pashtun. There is also a group of Pashtun called the Kuchi, who are nomads.

◀ A Hazara man repairs shoes on a street corner in Mazar-e Sharif. The Hazaras are generally not treated well by the other ethnic groups in Afghanistan.

The Tajiks speak Dari (Afghan Persian), the other official language of Afghanistan. They are closely related to the people of Tajikistan, and live in the valleys north of Kabul and in the region of Badakhshan. The Hazaras live in the centre and north of the country. Many Hazaras speak a unique dialect of the Persian language, with some Mongolian and Turkish vocabulary, but those in the major cities speak Dari.

The Hazaras have been discriminated against by the other groups and by successive governments, partly because they look different from other Afghans. The Uzbeks are the largest of a number of groups who speak Turkic languages. They live to the north of the Hindu Kush, near the Amu Darya River.

▼ In 1996 a group of Northern Alliance fighters walk along a road near Bagram. The Northern Alliance was mainly made up of Tajiks and Uzbeks who united to fight against the rule of the Taliban.

Did you know?

The oriental appearance of the Hazaras means that many people think they are descended from the Mongols. Others say their ancestors came from the Xinjiang region of north-western China. The Hazaras themselves believe that they were the original inhabitants of the region, the Buddhists who built the Bamiyan Buddhas.

Population data

- Population: 32,738,376
- Population 0-14 yrs: 44.6%
- Population 15-64 yrs: 53%
- Population 65+ yrs: 2.4%
- Population growth rate: 2.6%
- Population density: 50.6 per sq km/131.0 per sq mile
- Urban population: 23%
- Major cities: Kabul 3,277,000

Source: CIA

▲ Most Afghan people live in rural areas like this farmland region in Jabul-Saraj. Mud-brick houses can be seen among the terraced fields of crops.

THE FAMILY AND THE VILLAGE

Seventy-six per cent of people in Afghanistan live in villages. The family is ruled by the male head of the household, and several generations may live together in a mud-brick house or compound (small settlement of houses). Most villages have fewer than one hundred houses. The basic unit of social organization is known as the *qawm*, a grouping based on kinship and on where people live, but not necessarily on their ethnic group. Each village has three sources of authority: the *malik* (village headman), the *mirab* (master of the water distribution), and the *mullah* (religious leader or teacher). Often a *khan* (a word that means 'large landowner' but also means 'king') takes on the role of both *malik* and *mirab*. These roles are always occupied by men.

TOWNS AND CITIES

Only about a quarter of Afghanistan's population lives in the cities, although it is predicted that half the population will be doing so by 2050. The country's only major conurbation is Kabul, the capital, which has a population of about three million people. Kabul was founded over 3,000 years ago. Other major cities include Herat, Jalalabad, Mazar-e Sharif and Kandahar. Many ancient structures in Kabul, Herat and Kandahar were reduced to rubble during the wars, as were many new buildings. Unemployment and the high cost of housing have made life difficult for many city dwellers.

Focus on: Kabul

People from all over Afghanistan live in Kabul, the country's largest city. It has a population of between 2.5 and 4 million people. It is situated in the mountains, about 1,800 m (5,900 ft) above sea level, in a valley along the Kabul River. The area around Kabul has one of the highest densities of landmines in the world and has suffered badly from the many years of war.

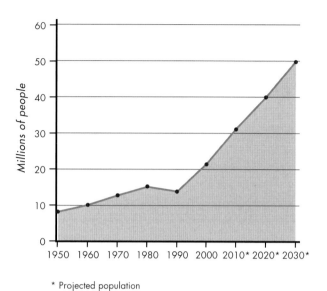

* Projected population

▲ Population growth, 1950-2030

▼ People returning to Kabul after years of war and instability are building new homes in the outskirts of the city.

CHAPTER 5

Government and Politics

Afghanistan is led by President Hamid Karzai, who was elected in October 2004 in the first presidential elections to take place since 1969. A Pashtun, who speaks several Afghan languages, Karzai had already been chosen as interim president by the US government in 2002 until elections could be held. In 2004, more than ten million Afghans registered to vote. Many potential candidates refused to stand, claiming that the elections were fraudulent. An independent commission did find evidence of fraud, but said that it had not affected the results. Karzai won 55.4 per cent of the vote. His cabinet includes members of the Northern Alliance, who fought alongside the USA in 2001. It also includes other representatives from the Loya Jirga, or Grand Council.

THE CONSTITUTION

In 2004, a new constitution established Afghanistan as an Islamic republic where men and women have equal rights and duties before the law. The USA held the power of veto (could make the final decision) over the document. Under the constitution, the government of Afghanistan has a president, two vice presidents, a Lower House (the Wolesi Jirga which means 'House of the People'), an Upper House (the Meshrano Jirga, which means 'House of the Elders'), and an independent

▼ Hamid Karzai (on the left), who was elected president of Afghanistan in 2004, speaks to the media while US President George W. Bush listens at the White House, Washington DC, in January 2002.

legal system. Mohammed Zahir Shah, the former king, returned to the country in 2002 but does not have any power.

PARLIAMENT

The Wolesi Jirga that was elected in September 2005 includes former Taliban members, warlords and *mujahideen*. There are also 68 women out of a total of 249 members of parliament (MPs). The population of each of the country's 32 provinces elects MPs to serve five-year terms. At least two women must be elected from each province.

The Meshrano Jirga consists of 102 members, a third of whom are voted in by provincial councils for a term of four years. A further third are elected by the district councils of each province for a term of three years. The final third are appointed by the president for five years. Half of the members of the Meshrano Jirga must be women.

Focus on: The Loya Jirga

'Loya Jirga' is a Pashtun term meaning 'Grand Council'. It is a traditional gathering of elders from the different groups in Afghanistan who come together to settle disputes. It dates back many centuries and is similar to the Muslim *shura,* or consultative assembly. The most famous Loya Jirga took place in Kandahar in 1747, when Pashtun tribal chiefs met to elect a king. After nine days, they still could not agree. The story goes that they chose the only man who had not spoken a word. His name was Ahmad Shah Durrani, and he went on to establish Afghanistan as a nation. The 2002 Loya Jirga included 2,000 delegates, 1,051 elected members, 100 seats for Afghan refugees, six seats for internally displaced Afghans and 25 seats for nomads. For the first time, 160 seats were reserved for women. The 2003 Loya Jirga, which took until 2004 to establish the new constitution, was nicknamed the 'loya jagra', or 'big fight', because there were so many disputes.

▶ People gather at a meeting to elect members of the Loya Jirga in Mazar-e Sharif in December 2003. A proportion of the elected places are reserved for women now that the Taliban regime has been removed.

THE LEGAL SYSTEM

The legal system under the new constitution consists of the Stera Mahkama (Supreme Court), appeals courts and lower district courts. Nine judges appointed by the president (and with the approval of the Wolesi Jirga) make up the Stera Mahkama, which has a ten-year term. Judges must be at least 40 years old. They must not belong to a political party and they must have a degree in law or Islamic jurisprudence. One of them is appointed chief justice. A separate Afghan Independent Human Rights Commission is responsible for investigating human rights abuses and war crimes.

The Stera Mahkama is the ultimate legal body, but it still has very conservative religious views. For example, in October 2005, Ali Mohaqiq Nasab, the male editor of a women's rights magazine, *Haqooq-i-Zan*, was jailed for two years after being convicted of blasphemy for publishing 'anti-Islamic articles'. These included a piece that challenged the belief that Muslims who convert to other religions should be stoned to death. The Stera Mahkama has also banned women from singing on television and called for an end to cable television.

SECURITY

Security remains an important issue. The government does not have power in many parts of the country, which are still controlled by warlords in charge of a total of around 50,000 armed militiamen. In contrast, the Afghan national army has just 14,000 troops. The International Security Assistance Force (ISAF)

▼ Ali Mohaqiq Nasab (second from right) is arrested on charges of blasphemy. On 21 December 2005, the Kabul High Court allowed Nasab to be released from jail after reducing his two-year sentence to six months.

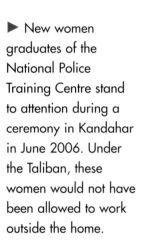

▶ New women graduates of the National Police Training Centre stand to attention during a ceremony in Kandahar in June 2006. Under the Taliban, these women would not have been allowed to work outside the home.

currently numbers about 50,700 troops from 41 NATO and non-NATO troop contributing countries. ISAF was created in December 2001 after the removal of the Taliban and has been controlled by NATO since 2003. Other foreign troops remain in the country to search for members of the Taliban and Al-Qaeda. There are 19,000 US soldiers, who were joined in spring 2006 by an additional 3,600 British troops. They are charged with the extremely difficult task of rooting out the opium trade and have also been involved in fierce fighting against Taliban militias. Despite the presence of these troops, violence has escalated. At least 1,400 people died in 2005 – the highest number since 2001.

Focus on: Women in politics

There is still considerable conservative opposition to women taking part in politics. Only a very brave woman chooses to become an MP in a country where many women and girls are still afraid to leave home without the all-covering *burqa* because they face violence and harassment on the streets. Many men still think women should stay at home. When two women parliamentarians travelled with a delegation to London, UK, without their husbands, some of the other male delegates said this should have been forbidden.

 Did you know?

The new political system in Afghanistan means that women form 25 per cent of the total number of parliamentarians, one of the highest proportions in the world. But an index measuring inequality between men and women puts Afghanistan above only one country in the world – Niger – so it is debatable as to how much power women actually wield.

Energy and Resources

Afghanistan is rich in resources, including natural gas, petroleum, coal, copper, chromite, talc, barites, sulphur, lead, zinc, iron ore, salt, and precious and semi-precious stones. However, the mountains, the history of conflict and lack of transport have meant that these resources are difficult to exploit.

GEMSTONES

The north-eastern regions of Afghanistan are some of the most important gem-producing areas of the world. The Hindu Kush is the western end of a gem-producing region that stretches along the Himalayas. Lapis lazuli, emeralds from the Panjshir Valley, green, blue and pink tourmaline, kunzite, and some rubies from the area between Jalalabad and Kabul have been found. But these treasures are difficult to extract and transport: for example,

rough-cut Panjshir emeralds must be taken on foot to northern Pakistan, a journey of some 200 km (124 miles) which can take up to 20 days through mountains seeded with landmines. The emeralds are then bought by Pakistani or Western buyers and taken away to be cut and sold.

COAL, OIL AND NATURAL GAS

The region around the Caspian Sea, to the north of Afghanistan, was estimated to have reserves of up to 49 billion barrels of oil and 232 trillion cubic feet of natural gas in 2008. Gas reserves in Turkmenistan are estimated to be the fifth largest in the world and Kazakhstan is

▼ This man is checking the purity of the emerald he holds in his fingers at a gemstone auction near Bazarak in 1999.

expected to become one of the world's largest oil producers. Afghanistan is not yet producing oil, though some people say that it has similar huge potential.

Natural gas was discovered in Afghanistan in 1967. After the Soviet invasion in 1979, between 70 and 90 per cent of the gas was directed to the Soviet Union's natural gas grid. In the 1980s natural gas accounted for 56 per cent of Afghanistan's export revenues. But after the Soviets left, the natural gas fields were capped. In 2005, Afghanistan produced an estimated 11.5 billion cubic metres (406.1 billion cubic feet),

although it is estimated that there are still 47.53 billion cubic metres (1.68 trillion cubic feet) of natural gas reserves in existence.

 Did you know?

Almost half of Afghanistan's energy comes from firewood.

▶ Coal is loaded on to a mule before being taken to Kabul. The years of war have meant that Afghanistan's energy supplies have been badly disrupted.

Focus on: The Koh-i-Noor diamond

The Koh-i-Noor ('Mountain of Light') diamond is said to be 5,000 years old and was originally supposed to have weighed 793 carats. Hindus claim that it was stolen from their god, Krishna. It was acquired by the Moghuls in 1526. The story goes that, in 1739, the Moghul emperor, Mohammed Shah, kept it hidden in his turban. The Persian king, Nadir Shah, engineered a public swapping of turbans, which the emperor could not refuse, and so Nadir Shah acquired the jewel. When Nadir Shah was assassinated in 1747, General Ahmad Shah Abdali took the diamond to Kabul and passed it to his son and

grandson, Shah Shuja, who became king. When he was deposed in 1813, Shah Shuja is supposed to have given it to Maharajah Ranjit Singh, governor of Lahore, who freed him from prison. The diamond was then lost until, in 1849, the British found it in the treasury in Lahore, Pakistan, and it was presented to Queen Victoria. She had it recut, reducing the weight from 186 carats to 108.93 carats, and it became part of the British Crown Jewels. Since then, many groups from Afghanistan, including the Taliban, have tried to reclaim the diamond. But until this day, it remains in Britain.

▲ A woman and her child at home in Kabul in 2005. They have a fan and a radio, but have to use a lantern for lighting as the electricity supply is often cut off. This situation applies to many ordinary Afghan people.

Afghanistan is estimated to have 66.2 million tonnes (65.2 million tons) of coal reserves, most of which are in the north of the country. Coal has been discovered in the Hindu Kush, in Karkar and Eshposhteh in Baghlan province, and in Fort Sarkari in Balkh province. In 2002 coal production had fallen to just 907 tonnes (893 tons) a year, but by 2006 had increased to almost 90,000 tonnes (88,600 tons) a year - similar to in the early 1990s.

ELECTRICITY

Afghanistan has considerable potential for hydro-electric power and there are dams and hydro-electric stations on the Kondoz, Kabul, Arghandab and Helmand rivers. But in the

conflict before and during the Taliban years and during the US-led invasion in 2001, transmission lines were brought down, turbines and floodgates blown up and, as a result, hydro-electric

Energy data

- ▱ Energy consumption as % of world total: n/a
- ▱ Energy consumption by sector (% of total)

Industry:	n/a
Transportation:	n/a
Agriculture:	n/a
Services:	n/a
Residential:	n/a
Other:	n/a

- ▱ CO_2 emissions as % of world total: 0.004
- ▱ CO_2 emissions per capita in tonnes p.a.: 0.0

Source: World Resources Institute

production almost stopped. It is now starting up again. In January 2003, the North-west Kabul Thermal Power Station was recommissioned after lying inactive for 14 years. This alone has almost doubled the available power supply in Kabul, which is particularly critical during the winter months, when demand increases by one-third.

In addition, several diesel generators have been installed in smaller provincial cities throughout the country, which had little or no access to electricity, including Faizabad, Baghdis, Bamiyan, Samanghan and Uruzgan. Some electricity is imported from neighbouring countries: the cities of Herat, Mazar-e Sharif and Kunduz have forged agreements with neighbouring Iran, Uzbekistan and Tajikistan to import energy. Even so, only around 6 per cent of Afghanistan's people have access to electricity. Ismail Khan, former warlord and now Afghanistan's energy minister, is optimistic that Kabul will have full power by the end of 2008.

Focus on: Pipelines

Many countries have had their eye on the oil under the Caspian Sea for some time. Russian and German companies wanted to build a pipeline through Eastern Europe, but this plan was abandoned when the former Yugoslavia was bombed during the 1990s. Russia and China have also negotiated with Iran and Kazakhstan about constructing a pipeline. In 1998, a consortium led by the American oil company, Unocal, started negotiations with the Taliban about a pipeline through Afghanistan, but the plans failed. In 2002, the Afghan government signed an agreement with Pakistan and Turkmenistan to take gas from Turkmenistan through Afghanistan to India and Pakistan. Villages along the route would be supplied with gas and the Afghan government would be paid for the gas passing through the country and would own the pipeline in 30 years' time.

▶ A section of pipeline near Mazar-e Sharif. It carries gas supplies from Turkmenistan through Afghanistan to India and Pakistan.

CHAPTER 7

Economy and Income

Afghanistan is an extremely poor country. Eighty per cent of its people are farmers, often growing only enough food for themselves and their families. Two-thirds of the people live on less than two US dollars a day and more than half of the population lives below the poverty line. The legacy of war and continuing conflict makes it difficult for things to improve. In 2008 Afghanistan still ranked the lowest of all 177 countries listed in the Human Development Index by the United Nations Development Programme.

Economically, Afghanistan is still very dependent on foreign aid, which amounts to 3.9 times the national revenue and accounts for 8 per cent of Gross Domestic Product (GDP). According to the World Bank, Afghanistan's operating budget for 2005 was $600 million.

Half of this came from taxes and the other half from international donors. It is estimated that Afghans living outside the country invested US$3 billion in the country (out of an economy with a GDP of around US$6-$7 billion).

PRODUCE, IMPORTS AND EXPORTS

Afghanistan produces wheat, fruits, nuts, wool, mutton, sheepskins, lambskins, soap, furniture, shoes, fertilizer, cement, textiles and hand-woven carpets. Karakul sheep are raised in large numbers in the north. The tight, curly fleece of Karakul lambs is used to make Persian lamb coats. In addition the country produces unusually sweet grapes and melons, grown mostly in the west, north of the Hindu Kush, and in the fertile regions around Herat.

◀ In May 2006 a man with oxen ploughs a field on his family farm. Many Afghans are farmers, but it is a hard life.

Focus on: Carpets

Afghan rugs and carpets are famous throughout the world. Those made by Turkmen and some Uzbeks are usually dark red with geometric figures, while the Baluchi make prayer rugs. Afghan carpets are made of wool, camel-hair or cotton.

▼ In April 2006 women weave a rug in the village of Boi Temur. Rug-weaving is one way in which women can earn money for themselves and their families.

 Did you know?

In September 2002, Afghanistan replaced its 'Old Afghani' notes with 'New Afghani' ones which were worth 100 times as much as the old. The old currency had been devalued so many times it had become almost worthless. Afghan people still use US dollars and currencies from neighbouring countries. This is because they believe they can rely on other, more stable currencies not to lose their value.

Economic data

- Gross National Income (GNI) in US$: 10,137,000,000
- World rank by GNI: 114
- GNI per capita in US$: less than 825
- World rank by GNI per capita: not specified but estimated to be below 210th
- Economic growth: 11.5%

Source: World Bank

In 1975, Afghanistan was self-sufficient in wheat, and grain was its main export. However, between 1998 and 2001, years of drought and then war resulted in poor or non-existent harvests. Today Afghanistan only produces enough to feed half its population, and imports eight times more goods than it is able to export.

SMUGGLING

For many years, governments of Afghanistan have profited from the trade in illegal goods across the country's borders. Televisions, cigarettes, guns and drugs all passed through Afghanistan on their way to Pakistan or Iran. In this way, the traders avoided paying the high taxes imposed by other countries, and the governments of Afghanistan received a share of the profits. A United Nations study estimated that, in 2000, 'unofficial' exports from

Afghanistan to Pakistan and Iran were worth US$941 million and US$139 million respectively. The Taliban was said to have made between US$36 million and US$75 million in this way. This was despite the fact that they had placed an official ban on consumer goods in Afghanistan.

OPIUM

Today Afghanistan's main trade is in opium, and the country is the world's largest producer of this drug. The red opium poppy was supposedly introduced to Afghanistan by

▼ Under the Taliban, TVs, radios and computers were not allowed to be brought into Afghanistan from other countries. Despite the ban, people made their own consumer goods, like these satellite dishes in a Kabul market, and smuggling was widespread.

▲ A farmer watches as his poppy crop in Kandahar is destroyed by officials using a tractor and plough. Despite efforts by the authorities to stamp out poppy production, farmers can make more money from this illegal crop than from growing anything else.

Alexander the Great (356-323 BC). Opium comes from the unripe seed heads, and is quick to produce and easy to transport. It offers an important source of income, especially to poor farmers who can make about US$5,200 from an acre of opium but only US$121 from an acre of wheat. Recent efforts to stamp out opium growing have not been successful, partly because the money from the opium trade is crucial not only to the farmers but also to maintaining the power of the warlords and to the country itself. The International Monetary Fund (IMF) estimates that between 40 and 60 per cent of Afghanistan's GDP comes from trade in opium. Between 80 and 90 per cent of

Europe's heroin comes from Afghan poppies. Between 2001 and 2005, the number of provinces producing opium increased from just six to 28 (out of a total of 32 provinces) and its export value was US$2.3 billion. Afghanistan's opium harvest was predicted to increase by nearly 60 per cent in 2006.

Did you know?

Afghanistan's central bank was founded in 1938. It issues notes, is in charge of government loans and lends money to cities and other banks.

CHAPTER 8

Global Connections

Despite its difficult terrain, Afghanistan has always had connections with other parts of the world. Its people have seen conquerors come and go, and they have traded with the many countries on their borders. Afghanistan was crossed by the famous Silk Route, an 8,000-km (5,000-mile)-long network of interconnecting roads which, between 500 BC and AD 1500, was the main route between Europe, the Near East, India and China. During this time, exotic and commercial goods, skills, knowledge, and religion – as well as silk, and explorers like Marco Polo – crisscrossed the European and Asian continents, and shaped the course of their histories and cultures.

REFUGEES

The conflict of the past 27 years has seen thousands of Afghan people fleeing abroad, mostly to Iran and Pakistan but also to the West. After Palestinians, Afghan people make up the largest number of refugees and internally displaced persons in the world. Since 2001, the United Nations has been able to bring back more than 3.5 million people, mainly from Pakistan and Iran, and some of them are playing an important role in the reconstruction of their country. But many do not feel safe to return, and more than two million refugees remain abroad. There are also between 167,000 and 200,000 people who are internally displaced in the south and west of Afghanistan itself.

▼ People wait at the Chaman border crossing into Pakistan in November 2001. Pakistan closed its border with Afghanistan to deter the numbers of refugees fleeing the country because of war.

▲ Men rebuild homes on the Shomali Plain outside Kabul. Many homes are being rebuilt after decades of war.

FORGING LINKS

More than 20 years of war have left Afghanistan not only poor, but also cut off from the rest of the world. Rebuilding of the country's roads, transport systems and communications is crucial to its reconstruction. But rebuilding its links with other countries and its trading partnerships is also very important. International aid is still a major part of the country's income. In 2007, Afghanistan's main export partners were India, Pakistan, the USA and Russia, while its main import partners were Pakistan, the USA, India and Germany. Some of these countries, such as Germany, have sizeable communities of Afghan refugees.

 Did you know?

There is a sizeable Afghan community in Guyana, South America. Afghans first arrived there more than 150 years ago.

Focus on: The Land of the Afghans

The various peoples who have come from different countries to rule Afghanistan over the years have given it many different names. One theory says that the name 'Afghanistan' comes from the alternative name for the Pashtun rulers, the *Afghans*, and the Persian word *stan*, meaning 'country' or 'land'. Another theory is that the word came from an ancient people known as *Ashvakas*, or the 'horse people'. One of the first names for the area was *Ariana*, the Greek version of the ancient *Aryanam Vaeja,* or 'Land of the Aryans'. The first Persian conquerors called the region the Province of Khorasan.

In 2006, Afghanistan's exports were worth US$274 million, while its imports amounted to US$3,823 million. Its main exports are opium, fruits, nuts, hand-woven carpets, wool, cotton, hides and pelts, precious and semi-precious gems. Its imports include capital goods (such as machinery and tools), food, textiles and petroleum products.

REGIONAL CO-OPERATION

In December 2005, Afghanistan hosted a regional economic co-operation conference, involving 12 countries, including the six that share borders with Afghanistan, plus India, Turkey, the United Arab Emirates, Kazakhstan and Kyrgyzstan. The conference aimed to promote economic co-operation in areas including electricity and energy generation, transport, trade, border management and investment.

The years of conflict have left the people of Afghanistan in need of training to update their skills. A number of projects (for example the Kabul Distance Learning Centre, see box opposite) have been set up to train teachers, midwives, journalists and civil servants and to link people via the Internet and email. The World Bank has set up a project that aims to improve performance at ten of the country's universities through partnership programmes with universities in other countries.

 Did you know?

Abdul Ahad Mohmand was the first Afghan cosmonaut (the Soviet term for astronaut). Before he became an cosmonaut, Mohmand served in the Afghan Air Force. In 1988, he spent nine days in space aboard the Russian Mir space station.

Focus on: Al-Qaeda and training camps

Since the Soviet invasion, young Muslim men have been taught how to fight using guerrilla tactics at military training camps in Afghanistan. Under the Taliban, military camps in Afghanistan, some of them run by Al-Qaeda, attracted an estimated 70,000 young Muslims from around the world. Here the men were given basic training for a number of weeks or months in the use of arms and explosives. They were also taught the Taliban's and Al-Qaeda's brand of anti-Western Islamic philosophy.

▶ A man who used to be a Taliban fighter shows a leaflet offering a reward for information to help with the capture of Al-Qaeda leaders Ayman al-Zawahiri (pictured on the left of the leaflet) and Osama Bin Laden (on the right).

Focus on: The Kabul Distance Learning Centre

In November 2002, a distance learning centre, supported by the World Bank, was established in Kabul. It is now used to assist with the sharing of development knowledge between people in Afghanistan and their counterparts around the world through new information and communications technologies. The centre's first video conference connected experts in Tajikistan, Kazakhstan, Uzbekistan and the USA to discuss development prospects in Afghanistan. Through the centre, Afghanistan's government agencies and others have been connected to the Internet, and have access to email for the first time.

▶ Women learn computer skills at an education centre in Kabul. Information technology is opening up new opportunities for international co-operation and helps people to keep informed about the world around them.

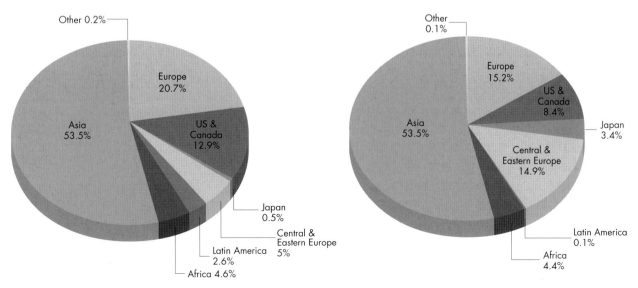

▲ Destination of exports by major trading region

Europe 20.7%
US & Canada 12.9%
Japan 0.5%
Central & Eastern Europe 5%
Latin America 2.6%
Africa 4.6%
Asia 53.5%
Other 0.2%

▲ Origin of imports by major trading region

Other 0.1%
Europe 15.2%
US & Canada 8.4%
Japan 3.4%
Central & Eastern Europe 14.9%
Latin America 0.1%
Africa 4.4%
Asia 53.5%

CHAPTER 9

Transport and Communications

Travel in Afghanistan is not easy, though there are plenty of nomadic people who trek many miles by foot every day. Most transport for ordinary people is either on foot or by donkey. In winter, the weather makes it impossible to travel or reach many parts of the country. Some roads have recently been repaired, but many are in a ruined state.

Although they existed in the past, there are no railways in Afghanistan today, other than a few kilometres of track across a bridge from

▼ In Kabul, two men use their own power to pull a cart loaded with firewood. The ruined Darulaman Palace can be seen in the background.

Transport & communications data

- 📁 Total roads: 34,782 km/21,617 miles
- 📁 Total paved roads: 8,229 km/5,115 miles
- 📁 Total unpaved roads: 26,553 km/16,499 miles
- 📁 Total railways: n/a km/n/a miles
- 📁 Airports: 12
- 📁 Cars per 1,000 people: 9.4
- 📁 Mobile phones per 1,000 people: 165
- 📁 Personal computers per 1,000 people: 4
- 📁 Internet users per 1,000 people: 21

Source: World Bank and CIA World Factbook

Focus on: The Salang Tunnel

At an altitude of 3,400 m (11,155 ft), the 2.7 km (1.7 mile) Salang Tunnel is one of the highest in the world. It connects the north and south of the country and links Afghanistan with Uzbekistan and Tajikistan. When the tunnel is open, it takes ten hours to travel from Kabul to the north of the country; when it is closed, the journey takes 72 hours. The Salang Tunnel was built by the Soviets in 1964. Its southern entrance and ventilation system were destroyed during fighting in 1998. In July 2004 it was opened for the first time since 1997. Work included reconstructing ventilation shafts and buildings and installing tunnel lighting, ventilation equipment and electric power generators. Since 2001, the tunnel has become a crucial link in the rebuilding of the country as a whole.

◀ A bus leaves the Salang Tunnel that reopened in 2004 after being rebuilt. The tunnel helps to connect Kabul with Mazar-e Sharif in the north of the country.

Uzbekistan. Barges loaded with goods navigate the Amu Darya River, which forms part of the border with Turkmenistan, Uzbekistan and Tajikistan. During their occupation, the Soviets completed a bridge across the Amu Darya and built the previously mentioned motor vehicle and railway bridge between Termez in Uzbekistan and Jeyretan in Afghanistan.

REBUILDING THE SYSTEM

An efficient transport system is essential for the delivery of aid, the rebuilding of the country's infrastructure and for helping Afghanistan get back on its feet. Since 2001, reconstruction projects have focused on rebuilding roads and improving transportation. Other projects include the opening, in January 2005, of a major road linking Afghanistan with Iran.

More than 970 km (603 miles) of rural roads are being improved, and a 389-km (242-mile) highway linking Kabul with Kandahar was opened in 2004.

THE MEDIA

Afghanistan's first newspaper was printed in 1875 and under Amanullah Shah (see page 10) the media flourished, but it was not a free press. In the 1950s, the government controlled 95 per cent of the media. The first radio station was opened in 1925, but it was destroyed in 1929 in the uprising against Amanullah Shah. Broadcasting only began again when Radio Kabul started transmitting in 1940.

After the 1978 coup, the press was suppressed and *shabnamah*, or 'night letters', containing uncensored news and opinions were secretly printed. Most other papers written by Afghans with news about their country were published outside Afghanistan. By the early 1990s, there were ten newspapers, but under the Taliban the media was even more strictly controlled and carried only government and religious information. Radio Kabul (which had become Radio Afghanistan in 1960) was renamed 'Radio Voice of Sharia', in line with the strict Islamic law, and television was banned.

In 2001, following the removal of the Taliban, the media returned. Radio Afghanistan was one of the earliest stations to restart, broadcasting the first music the country had heard in many years. Radio is the main medium in Afghanistan, and 85 per cent of the population have access to it. Today, many small privately run (as well as state run) radio stations broadcast regularly and there are at least ten television stations. Many of the leading presenters are former refugees. Restrictions on the media are still in place, however, and criticism of Islam is forbidden. In April 2005, Taliban radio was heard in Kandahar once again, supposedly broadcast using mobile transmission facilities.

TELEPHONES

There are still very few landline telephones in Afghanistan. There is only one telephone line for every ten people, and there are even fewer lines in rural areas. But the number of mobile phones is slowly growing. In 2003, two mobile phone companies

◀ A live interview is conducted on Aina women's radio station in Kabul. Aina is one of many small radio stations that have sprung up in Afghanistan now that the Taliban no longer controls the media.

started operating and there are now 5 million mobile phone users. Five VSATs (satellite connections) have been installed in Kabul, Herat, Mazar-e Sharif, Kandahar and Jalalabad, providing international and domestic voice and data connectivity. Two private mobile phone companies have been licensed to operate. Like urban young people everywhere, the youth of Afghanistan are keen to get connected. While Internet access is limited, in Kabul there are now Internet cafés as well as public 'telekiosks', where anyone can go online for a small fee.

❓ Did you know?

Afghanistan set up its Internet domain name www.af in 2003. This is now the Afghanistan government website.

▲ The main market in Mazar-e Sharif has a big board advertising telecommunications services. In Afghanistan, mobile phone and Internet use has gradually increased in recent years.

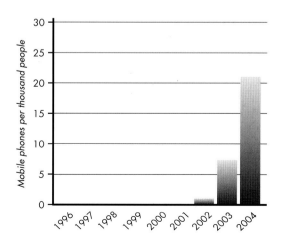

▲ Mobile phone use, 1996-2004

CHAPTER 10

Education and Health

About one in five Afghans is of school age. According to the World Bank, this is the highest ratio of school-age children to adults in the world, and it reflects the young average age of the population. From the late 1950s until the Soviet invasion in 1979, education in Afghanistan was valued highly and both boys and girls attended school and university. Kabul University had students from other parts of Asia and the Middle East. Following the Soviet invasion, military conflict made schooling difficult. Under the Taliban, boys generally received religious education in Islamic *madrasas*. These had always been an alternative to the school system and focused on the teaching of Arabic and the Koran, rather than basic skills. The Taliban forbade girls from going to school. As a result, the literacy rate, particularly among women, is one of the lowest in the world. Only 28 per cent of people over the age of 15 (51 per cent of men and 21 per cent of women) can read, write and do basic maths. In 2007, only 37 per cent of children went to primary school and, in some provinces, over 61 per cent of children were not enrolled. Nearly 80 per cent of the country's 6,900 schools had been damaged or destroyed in fighting during the Taliban years.

HIGHER EDUCATION

Under the Taliban, only a few students were able to go on to higher education. Of these, all were male and most of them studied religious subjects. At that time, only four universities were operational; by 2006, there were 14, including Mazar-e Sharif, Herat and Kandahar. Kabul has a number of universities and polytechnics and an institute of medicine. Women are now allowed to attend but, because so many missed out on education during the Taliban years, there are still not enough trained and qualified women teachers.

◀ In 2002 a schoolgirl in Agha Ali village, Kharaja, shows what she has learned. Under the Taliban, girls were not allowed to go to school, though some went to classes secretly.

THE SITUATION TODAY

In 2003, the 'Back to School' campaign launched by the Afghanistan interim government led to an estimated three million children and 70,000 teachers returning to school. But more than 70 per cent of schools still need repairs. Only half of the schools have clean water, and fewer than 40 per cent have adequate sanitation. In 2006, Taliban rebels carried out 99 attacks on schools and made 37 threats against schools and communities. The United Nations Children's Fund (UNICEF) reported that six children had died as a result of the violence.

Education and health

- Life expectancy at birth, male: 44.0 years
- Life expectancy at birth, female: 44.4 years
- Infant mortality rate per 1,000: 135
- Under five mortality rate per 1,000: 257
- Physicians per 1,000 people: 0.2
- Health expenditure as % of GDP: n/a
- Education expenditure as % of GDP: n/a
- Primary net enrolment: 37%
- Pupil-teacher ratio, primary: 83
- Adult literacy as % age 15+: 28%

Source: United Nations Agencies and World Bank

Focus on: Girls

Under the Taliban, girls were not allowed to go to school at all. Some attended illegal classes in one another's houses, at great risk to themselves and their teachers. Despite campaigns to get girls back to school since the end of Taliban rule, UNICEF estimates that more than one million of Afghanistan's primary school-age girls are still not enrolled. In five of the country's 32 provinces, 90 per cent of primary school-age girls do not attend school. The Afghan Ministry of Education and UNICEF have allocated US$19 million to help establish community based classes for up to 500,000 girls in villages and provide training programmes for 25,000 primary school teachers.

◄ Women at an adult literacy class in Hesarak village in northern Afghanistan. Under the Taliban, girls were not allowed to attend school so many women have never been taught to read and write. They must begin their education from scratch.

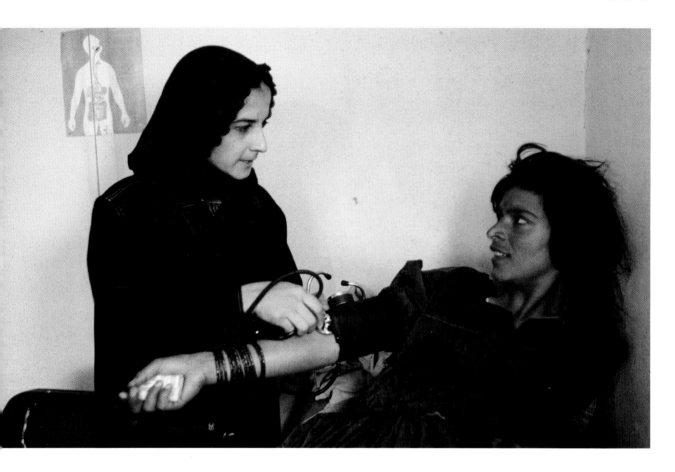

▲ A woman receives a check-up at a clinic for mothers and children. Many of the people seen at this clinic are being treated for the effects of living in a war zone.

HEALTH

The health of Afghanistan's people is one of the worst in the world. Life expectancy, at 44 years, is one of the lowest in the world – the average life expectancy for people living in low-income countries is 59. Afghanistan is at the bottom of all the 177 countries listed in the United Nations 2004 Human Development Report.

Infant and maternal mortality rates are also among the highest in the world. One in seven children dies in infancy, and one woman dies from pregnancy-related causes approximately every 30 minutes. Diseases that are no longer a problem in other countries are still very serious in Afghanistan. Thirty per cent of under five-year-olds are affected by diarrhoea. More than 60 per cent of all childhood deaths and disabilities in Afghanistan are the result of respiratory infections, diarrhoea and vaccine-preventable illnesses, especially measles. Tuberculosis and malaria are also common.

 Did you know?

The World Health Organization estimates that between 30 and 50 per cent of the population of a country experiencing conflict such as that in Afghanistan will find their mental health is affected. However, mental health problems are not being attended to because of the upheaval caused by the ongoing war and other pressing needs.

This situation of extreme poor national health is partly because only 13 per cent of Afghans have access to safe water, while 12 per cent have access to adequate water and sanitation, and 6 to 10 per cent have access to electricity. Sixty-five per cent have no way of getting to a clinic or accessing other healthcare. There are many landmines. This means there is a high risk of injury from stepping on one, and many victims die before they can reach a place where they can be treated. There is also a shortage of health workers, particularly women, which are essential in a country where most women want only to be treated by another woman.

WHAT IS BEING DONE?

In 2004, the US government donated US$83 million to improving health in Afghanistan. Nearly 7,575 health workers including midwives, doctors and nurses have been trained since then. UNICEF has organized mass vaccination programmes to immunize Afghan children against the most common diseases, and polio is close to being eradicated altogether. But it is a massive task; the whole health system needs to be constructed and the most basic elements are still not in place. Security, or lack

of it, makes it difficult to reach the most needy areas. In 2004, the international humanitarian aid organization Médecins Sans Frontières (Doctors Without Borders) withdrew from the country after five of its staff were killed in an ambush in the north of the country.

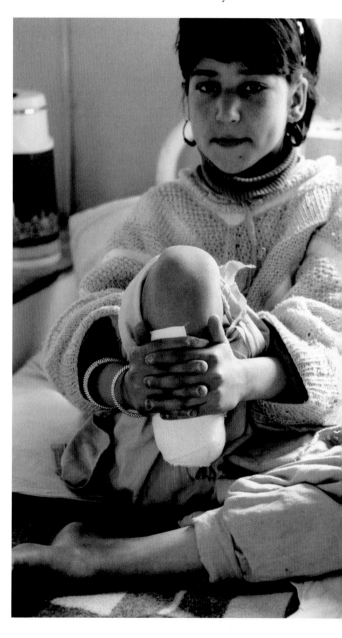

▲ This girl in a hospital in Kabul has had her foot amputated. Her injury was caused by stepping on one of Afghanistan's unexploded landmines.

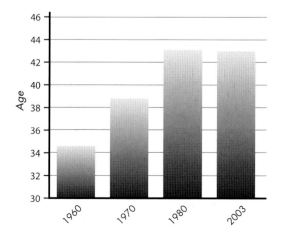

▲ Life expectancy at birth, 1960-2003

CHAPTER 11

Culture and Religion

For many thousands of years, Afghanistan was a crossing point for conquerors and traders and many of them left their treasures and part of their heritage behind. The country still has some beautiful, ancient buildings, priceless artworks and precious gemstones, though a number of them were looted or destroyed during the years of conflict. Coins dating from the eighth century BC and from countries as far apart as India, Italy, Egypt and Greece have been found in Afghanistan. The two beautiful mosques of Herat and Mazar-e Sharif are world famous. Other lesser known but equally remarkable sites include the 1,000-year-old Great Arch of Qal'eh-ye Bost, the Chel Zina (Forty Steps) and rock inscriptions made by the Moghul emperor Babur in Kandahar, the 'Towers of Victory' in Ghazni, Emperor Babur's tomb and the great Bala Hissar fortress in Kabul. Many ancient treasures were housed in the Kabul Museum, but this was bombed in 1993 and then looted by the Taliban. Items taken from the collection still turn up from time to time in different parts of the world.

Afghanistan has a long history of arts and crafts, and many are still practised today. For example, Herat is famous for its blue-green tiles and craftsmen there still make gold and silver jewellery, embroidery, rugs, carpets and leather goods.

▼ This beautiful mosque in Mazar-e Sharif is a shrine to Hazrat Ali, cousin and son-in-law of the Prophet Mohammed.

Focus on: The Bamiyan Buddhas

The two enormous Buddhas of Bamiyan were thought to date back to the third century. They were 53 m (175 ft) and 36 (120 ft) high and were the tallest standing Buddhas in the world. The Taliban blew them up in 2001 because they believe that all representations of human figures are anti-Islamic. There is now a plan by the Japanese artist Hiro Yamagata to create a laser projection of the original Buddhas on the site, using solar energy.

MUSIC

Afghans have always loved music. *Klasik* is Afghanistan's classical musical form, and there are at least 14 different instruments native to Afghanistan. They include the *tabla* (drums), a two-stringed instrument called the *damboura*, the *chang* (a plucked mouth harp), the lute-like *setar* and *sarang*, a type of flute called the *tula*, the *dilruba* (a bowed string instrument) and the *harmonya* (an accordion-style instrument). The *rabab*, or *rubab*, is another instrument a bit like a lute and is considered by some to be the national instrument. The singer Ahmad Zahir is one of Afghanistan's best-loved popular musicians and his music can even be listened to on the Internet. Ustad Mahwash is one of Afghanistan's best-known female singers and one of the few Afghan women to have trained with the classical masters. Safdar Tawakuli, a Hazara, is famous for playing the *damboura* and has been performing in Kabul now that the Taliban's ban on music has been lifted.

▲ Mirwais Najrabi, aged 13 (on the left) is accompanied on the Indian keyboard by his older brother, Nur-ul-Haq, in their Kabul home. Young male musicians are famous in Afghanistan. Their songs are now being heard once again after having been banned by the Taliban.

 Did you know?

The Taliban banned music, dance and singing; they also banned television, and punished anyone found watching it.

 Did you know?

The Minaret of Jam in western Afghanistan is the second-tallest brick tower in the world, after the Qutub Minar in New Delhi, India.

▶ This hairdressing salon in Kabul is doing good business now that Afghan women are allowed to go out of doors and dress fashionably again.

POETRY AND PHILOSOPHY

Afghanistan has always produced poets and philosophers, and its poetry often reflects the people's pride in their country. One of the most famous Afghan thinkers is Ibn-e-Sina-e-Balkhi (Avicenna of Balkh), who was born in Balkh in AD 980 and was a famous philosopher and scientist. Another is Jelauddin Rumi, a poet and founder of the Mawlawi Sufi Order, a leading mystical brotherhood of Islam.

CLOTHING

In the villages, men and women wear baggy cotton trousers. Men wear long cotton shirts, wide sashes around their waists, a skullcap and sometimes a turban on top. Women wear a long, loose shirt or dress, with a colourful swirling skirt over trousers, and wrap a shawl around their heads. The kinds of clothes people wear also depends on their ethnic grouping – Hazara women, for example, wear colourful red and green embroidered dresses over full trousers. In the cities, people's clothes vary much more, with some wearing traditional dress and others more modern clothes.

 Did you know?

For 800 years there was a small Jewish community in Afghanistan. At its largest it numbered around 5,000 people, but today only one Jewish person, Zablon Simintov, remains.

 Did you know?

The sacred cloak of the Prophet Mohammed is kept locked away in Kandahar. It is only displayed on very rare and special occasions. The Taliban leader, Mullah Omar, once famously showed it to the people in 1996. Until that point it had not been taken out for 60 years.

RELIGION

In Afghanistan, over 98 per cent of the people are Muslim. 89.2 per cent of the population are Sunni and 8.9 per cent are Shi'a (the majority of Hazaras are Shi'a). The remaining 1.9 per cent of the population includes Hindu and Sikh minorities, some of whom returned after the removal of the Taliban.

As Islam is the dominant religion in the country, the people of Afghanistan celebrate the Muslim holidays such as Eid al-Fitr and Eid al-Adha in the same way as most other Muslims. They attend mosque, visit friends and family, and prepare special foods. These Muslim holidays are all based on the cycles of the moon, but other holidays, such as Norooz, are based on the sun's movements. Norooz is celebrated on 21 March, the spring equinox, when the sun appears for exactly 12 hours in the day. Jeshen, on 19 August, is Afghan Independence Day and commemorates the day that British rule finally ended following the Third Afghan War.

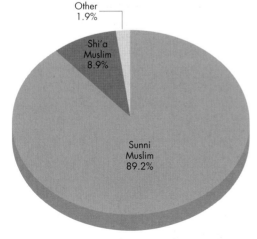

◀ A balloon-seller in Kabul waits for customers during the build-up to the Muslim festival of Eid al-Adha.

▲ Major religions

Other 1.9%
Shi'a Muslim 8.9%
Sunni Muslim 89.2%

 Did you know?

The beautiful fifteenth-century Blue Mosque at Mazar-e Sharif (see photo on page 46) is an important place of pilgrimage for Shi'a Muslims. It is believed to be the tomb of the Muslim leader Hazrat Ali, cousin and son-in-law of the Prophet Mohammed. In 1220 it was covered in earth to protect it from Genghis Khan and was only discovered again in the 1480s.

CHAPTER 12

Leisure and Tourism

There are many delicious traditional foods in Afghanistan, though today most Afghans have to eat what they can get hold of, especially in the countryside. Some dishes are similar to Persian, Asian or Middle Eastern ones, but there are many that are only found in Afghanistan, such as fried leek pastries called *boolawnee*, Afghani lamb with spinach, *samoos-i-yirakot* (stuffed vegetable turnovers) and Kabuli *pilau*, a dish of rice and chicken. The staple food is unleavened bread called *nan*. This is eaten with vegetables, fruit and rice and sometimes meat. Most people drink strong, black tea sweetened with a solid type of sugar that is rather like molasses.

Focus on: *Nan* bread

Nan is a traditional type of flat, unleavened bread also found in other countries in the region. In the countryside, it is baked on hot stones. In the cities, bakeries have circular fire-pits with cement walls. People take their homemade dough to be baked here. The baker rolls it out, makes little holes in it to keep it thin and puts it against the side of the fire-pit. The baker takes it out before it gets burned.

EXTREME SPORTS

The sport of *buzkashi* is unique to Afghanistan. The name '*buzkashi*' means 'goat killing'. The game is played on horseback and dates back many centuries. Only male stud horses are used in the game and they are specially trained. *Buzkashi* horsemen wear thick hats, quilted dresses, long boots and strong scarves wound

▼ This shop sells *nan* breads, a staple of the Afghan diet.

around their waists. The aim is to pitch a dead calf or goat across a goal line. The calf is beheaded, the legs cut off at the knee and the entrails removed. The carcass is then soaked in cold water for 24 hours before the game to make it tough. The game may last as long as a week and is accompanied by wrestling matches to prove the participants' strength. It is a very

▲ Men on horseback playing the traditional sport of *buzkashi*. The man in red is carrying the dead animal that has to be thrown across the goal line.

fast game and players are often injured. Other sports include soccer, played by every Afghan boy, and snowboarding.

Focus on: Kite flying

The people of Afghanistan like to fly kites, but not in a way that is like kite flying anywhere else. The sport of *Gudiparan bazi* (meaning 'flying doll') involves coating a kite wire with crushed glass and using it to try to cut the string of an opponent's kite and set it free. Kites come in all sizes, from miniature to ones as big as a person. They are made of thin paper and bamboo wood.

The wire is very important, and coating it in ground glass is a very complicated operation, which often involves severe cuts to the fingers. The wire is then wound round a drum. Most areas in a neighbourhood will have a *sharti* or kite flying champion. The Taliban banned kite flying, but it has recently been reintroduced.

▶ This woman is making colourful kites for the traditional sport of kite flying.

TOURISM

In the nineteenth and early twentieth centuries, many travellers came to Afghanistan. The author Robert Byron, who wrote *The Road to Oxiana* in 1933 about his travels in the region, said of the garden where he stayed in Kabul that it was: 'too pleasant to leave, full of sweet williams, Canterbury bells and columbines, planted among the lawns and terraces and shady arbours; it might be England until one notices the purple mountain behind the big white house.'

It is obvious that, with its rugged mountains and ancient treasures, Afghanistan without war would be a popular destination for tourists. Its first national park, Band-e-Amir, has several lakes of crystal-clear water, surrounded by towering red cliffs. Urial (a type of wild sheep) and ibex (wild goats) live here. The park meets the criteria for designation as a UNESCO World Heritage Site, but remains heavily mined from 2001 when it was the frontline between the Taliban and those opposing them. The Kole

Hashmat Khan wetland on the outskirts of Kabul was declared a waterfowl reserve by King Zahir Shah in the 1930s and in the 1960s supported tens of thousands of ducks, as well as wintering and migratory birds. But it has not been protected; many internally displaced people live there and its bird life has declined.

The 1970s were the height of tourism in Afghanistan, with some 90,000 visitors making a significant contribution to the country's earnings. Even under the Taliban there was a Minister of Tourism, although the Taliban's version of strict Islam did not encourage

 Did you know?

Afghanistan had its own unique way of marking the United Nations' 'Make Poverty History' campaign. More than 300 Afghan children flew white kites in September 2005 to say 'Don't forget us' to world leaders.

tourists. Today a few intrepid visitors are creeping back, but their safety is not guaranteed. The latest *Lonely Planet* guide to Central Asia now includes a section on Afghanistan. Despite Afghanistan's beauty, the US government website warns that it is currently too dangerous for US citizens to visit, and most foreigners in Afghanistan today are aid workers or journalists rather than tourists.

Tourism in Afghanistan

- Tourist arrivals, millions: n/a
- Earnings from tourism in US$: n/a
- Tourism as % foreign earnings: n/a
- Tourist departures, millions: n/a
- Expenditure on tourism in US$: 1,000,000

Source: World Bank

◀ In Kabul, the grounds and mosque of Baghe Babur date back to 1638 and have recently been reopened. Afghanistan has many beautiful ancient buildings like this that may become popular with tourists one day.

Focus on: Kabul Zoo

Humans suffered during the years of war in Afghanistan, and so did the animals at Kabul Zoo. There used to be 50 species of birds and animals at the zoo, but these were reduced to 16 during the war years when the zoo was closed. With the help of the World Society for the Prevention of Cruelty to Animals, the zoo has now re-opened. It has 100 animals, mostly from Afghanistan itself, and an education programme for children. As one of the few places of entertainment in the city, the zoo attracts up to 5,000 visitors at weekends. However, concerns were expressed about the treatment of the animals by some of the visitors when a bear and a deer died after being fed chewing tobacco.

CHAPTER 13

Environment and Conservation

Afghanistan's environment is harsh: the arid land and long, cold winters make it difficult for people, plants or animals to survive. In 2,000 BC, the country was covered with cedar-rich forests. But over the years its people were forced to cut down the forests for fuel in order to make a living, and their animals overgrazed the already fragile fields. As a result, the soil has been eroded by water and wind. The effects of irrigation, which has been practised over many years, mean that much of the land that might be suitable for cultivation – which in any case covers only 12 per cent of the country – has been made too salty for use. Only 6 per cent of the country's land is currently being used for farming.

POLLUTION AND WATER SHORTAGE

Water is scarce and often polluted by contamination from waste dumps, chemicals and open sewers. There is no proper rubbish collection in most cities and it is just dumped, resulting in a health hazard and sometimes causing groundwater pollution. Many deep wells have been drilled and these affect groundwater levels, including the traditional *karez* system of underground water canals.

? Did you know?

Although it does not have any significant industry of its own, the city of Kabul suffers from smog. This is partly because of the amount of firewood burned in a city with few other sources of light, heat or cooking fuel, and partly the result of vehicle emissions. Industrial parks in Iran, Turkmenistan and Uzbekistan also pump out emissions that pollute the air in Kabul.

◀ A woman and children collect water from a standpipe in the street. Many Afghan people have no access to clean water.

Between 1998 and 2002, four years of drought resulted in the Helmand River running as much as 98 per cent below its annual average. A United Nations study in 2002 found that more than 99 per cent of the Sistan wetlands, a critically important haven for waterfowl, had become completely dry. In the 1970s, before the Soviet invasion, the government, with the help of the UN and other agencies, began to try to deal with some of these problems. The country today has seven protected areas, though they cover less than 1 per cent of the land.

PLANTS AND TREES

Before the years of war, forest lands amounted to about two million hectares (about five million acres), or about 4.5 per cent of the country in eastern and south-eastern Afghanistan. Since 1978, almost 50 per cent of the country's forests have disappeared. Less

Focus on: Landmines

There are between five and seven million landmines in Afghanistan, most of them dating from the time of the Soviet occupation. Up to 150 people a month are injured, and more than 200,000 have been killed or injured by landmines over the past two decades. Many of these are children – for example, young shepherds tending their sheep. In May 2006, the Afghanistan government reported that since signing the Mine Ban Treaty in 2002 it had destroyed 65,973 stockpiled landmines. It is also slowly clearing existing landmines. So far, 7,000 Afghans have been trained in the dangerous work of de-mining. Legislation has been passed to give people with disabilities free medical care and a pension. But many warlords and militias still possess mines, as do neighbouring countries such as Burma (Myanmar), India, Nepal and Pakistan.

▼ A man searches for unexploded landmines. This is a delicate and dangerous operation. Clearing Afghanistan of landmines will take many years.

than 2 per cent of the country is now forested. Trees include various kinds of evergreens (including some ancient cedars), oaks, poplars, wild hazelnuts, almonds and pistachios. In the northern steppes and the south-western deserts, plants such as camel thorn, locoweed, spiny restharrow, mimosa and wormwood (a variety of sagebrush) flourish, despite the harsh conditions.

ANIMALS AND BIRDS

Despite its difficult terrain, more than 100 types of mammal manage to live in Afghanistan. Some of them, such as the goitered gazelle, leopard, snow leopard, markor goat and Bactrian deer, are in danger of dying out. Other wild animals include Marco Polo sheep, ibex, bears, wolves, foxes, hyenas, jackals, mongooses, wild boar, hedgehogs, shrews, hares, mouse hares, bats, and a variety of rodents. There are more than 380 bird species. Flamingo and other water birds breed in the lake areas south and east of Ghazni. Ducks and partridge are also common, but all birds are hunted widely and many are in serious danger of dying out, especially the Siberian crane.

CONSERVATION

In 2002, the Loya Jirga set up the Ministry for Irrigation, Water Resources and Environment to take the lead in ensuring that care for the environment was a part of the reconstruction process. Some of the money designated for Afghanistan by the international community is being used for the conservation of wildlife and the environment. For example, the Asian Development Bank (ADB) has promised US$1,785 million to protect plant and animal life in certain regions. The United Nations Environment Programme (UNEP), together with the European Commission and the Ministry of Irrigation, Water Resources and Environment (MIWRE), has promised US$5.15 million to support the rehabilitation of the country's environment. The United Nations Millennium Development goals for Afghanistan

Environmental and conservation data

- 🗁 Forested area as % total land area: 0.04
- 🗁 Protected area as % total land area: 0.3
- 🗁 Number of protected areas: 7

SPECIES DIVERSITY

Category	Known species	Threatened species
Mammals	119	13
Breeding birds	181	11
Reptiles	109	1
Amphibians	7	1
Fish	115	n/a
Plants	4,000	1

Source: World Resources Institute

◀ The snow leopard is one of the most endangered mammals in Afghanistan and in the world.

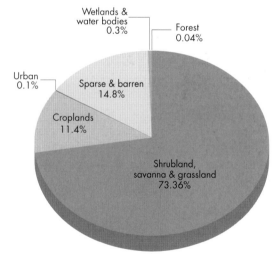 A young boy sells firewood from the back of his bike on the outskirts of Kabul. Many poor families have no choice but to burn precious wood for fuel.

include helping to make sure that any development that occurs does not destroy the environment, and reversing the loss of environmental resources by 2015. In January 2006, the government enacted the first environmental legislation, which aims to protect and conserve wildlife, waterways and forests.

However, despite fine words and promises of money, repairing the country's ravaged environment may take a long time. When the people have so little, protecting the environment for future generations comes second to the battle for daily survival, even if this includes cutting down precious trees to sell as firewood so that people and their children can eat.

▲ Types of habitat

(pie chart)
Wetlands & water bodies 0.3%
Forest 0.04%
Urban 0.1%
Sparse & barren 14.8%
Croplands 11.4%
Shrubland, savanna & grassland 73.36%

 Did you know?

The large, longhaired, silky Afghan hound, comes from Afghanistan! The first of these dogs was brought to Britain in the nineteenth century.

 Did you know?

In 1978, there were 70 endangered Siberian cranes in Afghanistan. By 2006, according to SAVE (the Society for Afghanistan's Viable Environment), there was only one pair with a chick left.

CHAPTER 14

Future Challenges

Afghanistan still faces many challenges. It remains a country in conflict. Rebuilding, forging political stability and security, reducing levels of poverty and raising life expectancy, improving the role of women, combating the drug trade – all these tasks remain to be done and none is going to be easy. The rate of violent crime is higher today than at any time since 2001. The gap between rich and poor is increasing, particularly in Kabul, where some people are making lots of money. Many refugees are returning from the West, and making big contributions to society, but they also bring different perspectives and experiences and are usually richer than those Afghans who remained in the country. This can cause tensions and resentment between these people and those who lived through the years of war in Afghanistan.

THE STRUGGLE FOR CONTROL

The government is not in control of parts of the country ruled by the warlords, and the Taliban fighters remain in the mountains and remote areas. Osama bin Laden and other Al-Qaeda leaders have still not been found, despite the thousands of foreign troops in the country looking for them. But there are some signs of hope. There is a new government in place, and a national parliament and legal system. Many people have been able to vote for the first time in their lives. Women are slowly returning to the public sphere, though many face intimidation and violence for doing so. Four million students are back in school. Healthcare is improving – for example, immunization campaigns have meant that incidences of polio and measles have fallen.

► These young girls are the first to be able to enjoy playing games openly now that the Taliban has fallen. However, schools have recently been attacked and the dangers are not yet over.

◀ British soldiers of the NATO-led International Security and Assistance Force (ISAF) patrol the streets of Kabul in July 2006.

To date, more than US$648 million have been pledged to the Afghanistan Reconstruction Trust Fund (ARTF) by 24 donor countries. If things are to improve, all the money promised needs to be delivered. Infrastructure must be improved so that transport systems function and electricity and clean water are delivered to the people. Education and health also need support and investment. The country needs to be made safe enough for Afghan refugees to return and the economy needs to be strong enough for them to be able to make a living again.

Above all, the Afghan people need to own what is happening in their country – from the government to local communities. This is not easy, as there are so many problems and international aid and foreign governments influence so much. A conference in London in February 2006 attended by representatives from almost 70 countries backed a peace plan and pledged resources to rebuild the country. But all agree that this will take time and will not be an easy task.

Did you know?

In Kabul there is a smart new shopping mall and a five-star hotel where rooms cost US$280 (£158) a night and the presidential suite is a princely US$1,225 (£690) per night.

Focus on: Child soldiers

Many young boys fought in Afghanistan's wars, both for the Taliban and against them. A UNICEF programme, started in February 2004, has so far helped 4,000 of these young people to find their way back into employment. With the help of local people they have trained in animal husbandry, motor mechanics, tailoring, masonry and carpentry. They are also given medical checks and education possibilities. Each former child soldier has to sign a pledge of good conduct, in which he agrees to help with the reconstruction of his country and promises not to return to fighting.

Timeline

329 BC Alexander the Great conquers Afghanistan and Persia.

AD 100 Kushan Buddhist Empire.

400 White Huns invade from the north and destroy Buddhist culture.

530 Persians gain control of the whole of Afghanistan.

650-1030 Islamic era established by invading Arabs. Ghaznavid and Ghorid dynasties continue after the Arabs leave.

1219-21 Genghis Khan invades.

1370 Tamerlane, or Timur, conquers Afghanistan.

1330? Ghorid dynasty re-establishes itself.

1504-19 Babur, a descendant of Timur, founder of the Moghul dynasty, takes control of Kabul.

1520 Afghanistan becomes part of the Moghul Empire, established in India under Timur's successors.

1550 Persian Empire takes over in the West.

1613-89 Khushhal Khan Khattak, Afghan warrior poet, starts a national uprising against the Moghul government.

1725 Mir Mahmud invades Persia.

1735 Persia drives back Mahmud, re-takes Kandahar.

1750-75 Under Ahmad Shah Abdali, Afghans liberate Kandahar, and drive the Moghuls back into India. Ahmad Shah establishes the Kingdom of Afghanistan.

1820s Britain and Russia both want control of central Asia.

1839-42 First Afghan War between British and Afghans.

1878 Second Afghan War. Khyber and Pischin conceded to the British.

1880 Battle of Maiwand. Abdul Rahman takes the throne with the help of the British who withdraw, retaining the right to handle foreign relations.

1920-21 Third Afghan War. Afghanistan gains independence from Britain.

1930-33 Nadir Khan takes the throne and founds a dynasty which rules until 1978.

1940 Zahir Shah declares Afghanistan neutral in the Second World War; kingdom retreats into isolation.

1953 Zahir Shah's cousin, Daoud Khan, becomes prime minister.

1959 In a modernization programme, women are allowed to enrol at universities and in the workforce.

1963 Zahir Shah usurps Daoud and gives limited powers to a parliament.

1973 Zahir Shah's government is overthrown in a coup headed by his cousin Daoud Khan, who abolishes the monarchy and declares himself president of the republic.

1978 Communist coup. Daoud is killed and Taraki is made president. He signs a treaty of friendship with the Soviet Union. The Afghan guerrilla (*mujahideen*) movement is born.

1979 Army massacres peasants. The US ambassador is killed, as are Taraki and his successor, Hafizullah Amin. Babrak Karmal takes power. The Soviet Union invades to fight the *mujahideen* and support Karmal. Covert CIA aid to *mujahideen* begins. Millions of Afghans flee to refugee camps in Pakistan.

1980-6 CIA provides $2 billion in military aid to *mujahideen*, who also turn to the heroin trade to fund their war.

1986 Soviets impose KGB-trained secret police chief Najibullah, who becomes president.

1988-9 Peace accords signed in Geneva. Soviet Union withdraws. *Mujahideen* continue to fight against Najibullah.

1992 *Mujahideen* take control of Kabul and declare an Islamic state under Burhanuddin Rabbani.

1994 Birth of the Taliban.

1996 Taliban force President Rabbani and his government out of Kabul and execute Najibullah. Taliban offer refuge to Osama bin Laden.

1999 United Nations Security Council imposes sanctions.

2001 9/11 terrorist attacks on the USA. The USA and its allies attack Afghanistan to get rid of the Taliban, Al-Qaeda and Osama bin Laden. The Bonn Agreement establishes an interim government with Hamid Karzai as its president.

2004 First presidential elections since 1969. Hamid Karzai is elected.

2005 Parliamentary elections are held.

January 2005-August 2006 64 suicide attacks take place.

May 2006 Several people are killed by a US military vehicle; violent protests against the USA take place in Kabul.

May-June 2006 Many die in battles between Taliban fighters and Afghan and coalition forces in the south of the country.

July 2006-present NATO troops take over the leadership of military operations in the south. Fighting continues with the Taliban. British troops in Helmand province are under constant bombardment.

September 2006 Safia Hama Jan, a leading women's rights figure and outspoken critic of the Taliban is murdered in the streets of Kandahar.

Glossary

Assassination The killing of a person for political reasons.

Burqa A garment covering a woman's whole body and face, leaving only a meshed panel for her eyes.

Central Intelligence Agency (CIA) The USA's national security intelligence agency.

Coalition An alliance of different countries or parties who agree to work or fight together.

Communism A political system in which power resides with a single party that controls all economic activities and provides services.

Controversy An argument or debate, especially one carried on in public or in the media.

Coup The overthrow of a ruler of a country often, but not always, by the military.

Covertly Secretly.

Democracy A political system in which each adult person has the right to vote and government is made up of elected representatives.

Ethnic A population group sharing a distinctive cultural and historical tradition, often associated with race, nationality or religion.

European Commission The branch of the governing body of the European Union (EU) which carries out its laws and administers some of its money.

European Union A union of 25 countries that aims to improve political, economic and social co-operation.

Gender The way in which a man or a woman is socially conditioned to behave in a certain way according to his or her sex.

Gross Domestic Product (GDP) The total market values of goods and services in a country.

Internally displaced person Someone who has had to leave his or her home for fear of persecution or natural disaster and who lives somewhere else in his/her own country.

International Monetary Fund (IMF) A United Nations agency which aims to promote trade and increase growth by stabilizing exchange rates.

Islamist A believer or follower of Islam.

Jurisprudence A system of law.

Loya Jirga The traditional governing 'Grand Council' of Afghanistan.

Madrasa An Islamic school where the Koran is taught by rote.

Militia An armed group, usually independent and not connected to a government.

Mujahideen Guerrilla fighters in an Islamic country supporting the cause of Islam.

Mullah A male religious teacher in Islam.

Nomad A person who traditionally does not live in one place but travels around with other nomads.

Nomadic Always moving from place to place.

North Atlantic Treaty Organization (NATO) A military alliance formed between the USA and several European countries following the Second World War. The aim of the alliance was to prevent a Soviet invasion of Europe.

Plateau A flat expanse of land at a high altitude.

Puppet king A nominal ruler who has little real power.

Refugee Someone who has been forced to leave his or her home country for fear of persecution on account of race, religion, nationality, membership of a particular social group, or political opinion.

Sharia law The Islamic code of law based on the Koran.

Shi'a Muslims Those Muslims who believe that religious authority lies with a direct descent of the Prophet Mohammed.

Steppes Vast, flat, treeless plains, usually covered in grass.

Sunni Muslims Those Muslims who believe that religious authority must lie with the person chosen by the religious community as their leader.

Tectonic plate A piece of the earth's crust. The earth has ten major tectonic plates and many small ones.

Terrorist Someone who systematically uses violence against civilians, usually to achieve a political goal.

Tribe Families, clans or other groups who share a common ancestry and culture.

United Nations An organization founded at the end of the Second World War, with the aim of preventing future wars. Today more than 190 nations belong to the UN.

United Nations Children's Fund (UNICEF) The United Nations organization that is responsible for children all over the world.

World Bank An international organization that lends money to poor countries.

World Health Organization (WHO) The United Nations organization that specializes in health around the world.

Zoroastrianism The religion founded by Zoroaster in the tenth century BC, which is based on the conflict between good and evil and has a particular reverence for fire.

Further Information

BOOKS TO READ

Afghanistan: A Land in Shadow
Chris Johnson
(Oxfam, 1998)

X

Afghanistan: A Modern History
Angelo Rasanayagam
(I B Tauris, 2003)

X

similar

A Short Walk in the Hindu Kush
Eric Newby
(Picador, 1958)

My Forbidden Face
Growing up under the Taliban: A Young
Woman's Story
Latifa
(Virago, 2002)

✓

The Road to Oxiana
Robert Byron
(Penguin, 1937)

The Sewing Circles of Herat
Christina Lamb
(Flamingo (HarperCollins), 2002)

✓

War Without End
Dilip Hiro
(Routledge, 2002)

X

The Kite Runner
Khaled Hosseini
(Bloomsbury, 2004)

✓

USEFUL WEBSITES

http://topics.developmentgateway.org/
afghanistan/rc/AllFolder.do
Short summaries and links to a range of studies
on different aspects of the country.

http://www.afghan-web.com
Daily updates and a wealth of background
information.

http://www.afghanistans.com
A very informative and accessible site with a
wide range of different sections.

www.unicef.org
Information and statistics particularly on
children in Afghanistan.

www.worldbank.org
Detailed statistical information and reports on
the role of the World Bank in the
reconstruction of the country.

https://www.cia.gov/library/publications/the-
world-factbook/geos/af.html
Facts and figures.

http://www.oxfam.org.uk/coolplanet/kidsweb/
world/afghan/index.htm
Clear, concise and great photos. Stories of
children's lives.

 + a thousad splendid suns.

Index

Page numbers in **bold** indicate pictures.

About the Author

Nikki van der Gaag is a freelance writer, editor and evaluator on development issues. She has held senior editorial posts in the voluntary and not-for-profit sector. She was editorial director at the Panos Institute, co-editor of *New Internationalist* magazine and Education Publications Manager with Oxfam GB.